MW00682218

Your Purebred Puppy

Miriam Fields-Babineau

T.F.H. Publications, Inc.
One TFH Plaza
Third and Union Avenues
Neptune City, NJ 07753

This book has been published with the intent to provide accurate and authoritative information in regard to the subject matter within. While every precaution has been taken in preparation of this book, the publisher and author assume no responsibility for errors or omissions. Neither is any liability assumed for damages resulting from the use of the information herein.

ISBN 0-7938-3090-7

Printed and bound in the United States of America

Printed and Distributed by T.F.H. Publications, Inc.
Neptune City, NJ

Contents

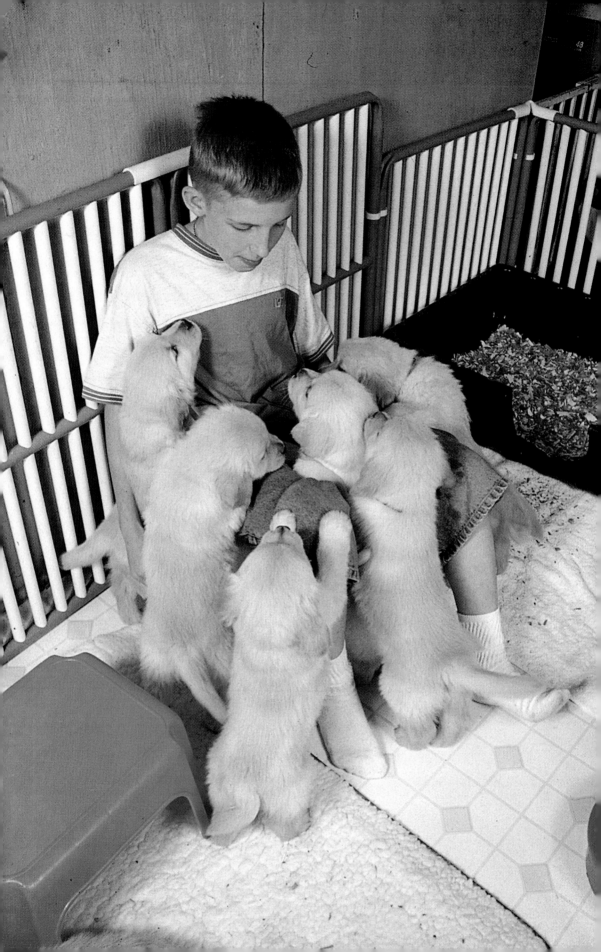

Which Breed Is For Me?

The breed of puppy you choose to own should not be a fashion statement. Your new family member will be a part of your life for upward of ten years. Choosing Simon, your purebred puppy, should be an honest and well-researched decision based on your personality and lifestyle. Fashion is fickle, but your relationship with your dog is long term. Make sure that the dog you choose will be a welcome addition to your life.

The first thing you should consider is the reason why you want Simon. Do you want a show dog, a hunting dog, a search and rescue dog, or just a pet? Many dogs are obtained with the original intention of being a family pet. If the dog has the appropriate breeding and training, he can quickly pick up any task that his owner desires. Keeping in mind what that ultimate goal is will help you make the final choice.

Regardless of what you intend to pursue with your new puppy, he will be a part of your family first and foremost. He needs to fit in and feel that he is a valued family member. Achieving these goals will require many hours of training and consistency from all involved. Is everyone in your family ready for this new responsibility? Can the breed you've chosen work well within your family structure and living conditions?

Before purchasing your puppy, there are a few things to consider. If you have children, you need to obtain a breed that interacts well with them. For example, an Australian Shepherd, because of his natural instinct to herd, may injure young children who are running and playing, or a terrier, because of his tenacious nature, may not recognize a child as an authority figure.

If you spend long hours away from home, you should not choose a high-energy breed, such as a sporting or working dog. A terrier also may not do well spending a lot of time alone. In fact, not many dogs will be happy if left alone for countless hours. If this is the case, you should rethink your purpose for obtaining a dog in the first place. If you wanted a dog to spend weekends in the woods with, then you may want to borrow a neighbor's pet or a dog from a rescue organization. Dogs require lots of socialization time with you and with other dogs, which means more than just ten minutes in the morning and two hours of company when you return home.

If you live in an apartment, condominium, or town home, you will need to devote much of your time to exercising your dog. Unless you can offer Simon several long walks a day with much of it in a safely enclosed, large area for free running exercise, definitely consider a smaller breed of dog or one that has a low energy level.

Ask yourself the following questions:

1. What is the dog's purpose? Will he be a show dog, hunting dog, watch dog, or just a companion?
2. How much time will you have for the dog? Dogs need to be fed, groomed, exercised, and trained, as well as taken on occasional trips to the veterinarian. You can count on your dog taking over an hour of your time per day, and this is not just time spent in his company. It's time of interaction with Simon where he is the center of your attention.
3. Is the new dog financially feasible? There is the initial cost of a purebred dog, which depends on the breed and quality, as well as the cost of food, veterinary treatment, grooming, bedding, license, parasite control, and kenneling if you go away. Some dogs, regardless of how carefully bred, are prone to chronic disorders, then there are the normal geriatric conditions associated with aging.
4. What is your housing situation? Do you live in a small or large home? What is the size of your yard? Do you have a fenced-in exercise area for the new dog? Are dogs allowed where you live?
5. What are the ages of your children? Some breeds do not coexist well with very young children, while others may not do well with active, older children.
6. Do you have elderly parents living with you? You do not want to bring home a bouncy young pup that jumps on people. The elderly or infirm are easily injured. A smaller or less active breed might be more appropriate.
7. Does any family member have allergies? You'll need to consider the dog's length of fur, dander, and shedding. While there are a few breeds that can be considered hypoallergenic, most are not. The last thing you want to do is fall in love with a dog and have to give it up due to a family member becoming ill.
8. Do you already have pets? While some dogs and cats will welcome another four-legged companion, there are many that won't. You'll need to make sure your current companions will be accepting of a new pack member.

In order to know which breed will be best for your family and lifestyle, you should read many books and visit with friends who own the breeds that interest you. A trip to a dog park or watching some obedience classes will also give you an idea of specific breed behavior. A great place to discover breeds that you may never have considered are dog shows. There are many different types of shows, from conformation, obedience, and agility to fieldwork. Watching the dogs in action will give you a better appreciation of their unique personalities and abilities.

A dog from the Sporting Group will be energetic, easily trained, generally good with children, and very social. These dogs are exceptional hunting companions, bred specifically to fill every

Make sure that you are ready for the responsibility of dog ownership before taking a puppy home.

niche in the hunting sport—pointing, flushing, retrieving, and locating. They also do well as pets, but due to their high energy levels, they require a lot of exercise and space. Sporting dogs should not be kept in a small home or confined to a small yard, which can make them destructive.

There are several subsections within this group that offer different personalities. Pointers tend to be a little more difficult to train and have a high energy level. If you obtain a pointer for hunting purposes, you'll live together harmoniously. Pointers do not, however, make the greatest pets unless you live a very active lifestyle.

Retrievers are known for their trainability, eagerness to please, and great social skills. They are the perfect family dogs, but do require a lot of exercise. These breeds cannot be confined to a small area for lengths of time without becoming destructive. It might not be a good idea to own a retriever if you have very young children, because they are generally exuberant greeters. They are, however, great for older children or anyone with an active lifestyle. These breeds can be great pets or working dogs.

Spaniels look like eternal puppies with their long, silky ears and round faces. They also act like puppies well into their adult years. With their long curly coats and big brown eyes, they can easily steal your heart. Keep in mind that they do require a lot of exercise, and a run in a field full of tall grass is just the thing. They spring and romp through a field with fervor, never slowing down until naptime. They're happy to fulfill the task of foot warmer for their napping people. Most spaniels are great with children of any age, but may not do well in a closed-in environment with people who either work long hours or are not active.

Spaniels are great hunting dogs, show dogs, and agility dogs. They are thrilled at the mere thought of a new adventure. There is one thing to consider, however. Most spaniels require professional grooming every six to eight weeks in order to remain in top condition. They are prone to ear infections and, if not properly groomed, can also get skin problems.

The Vizsla and Weimaraner don't fit into any sporting dog category, so they need to be addressed as individual breeds. Both require a lot of exercise, training, socialization, and observation and cannot be left in a kennel or at home for long periods of time by themselves. Vizslas can be reserved and should live in a quiet family. Weimaraners are outgoing and can thrive in a high-energy household with older children. However, beware that both breeds can be highly destructive if left alone. They are bred to be hunting dogs that point and retrieve all day, thus they have large amounts of energy and become bored easily.

Hounds come in so many shapes and sizes that one can hardly generalize their personalities. It is safe to say that most can be stubborn and more difficult to train than a sporting dog. Many hounds require a lot of exercise, training, and consistency and few are aggressive. Bred to locate prey, hounds tend to hone in on a scent and forget everything else going on around them. For this reason, they should never be allowed to run free in an area that is not fenced. Exercising them in a closed-in baseball field would be ideal. Hounds are generally quiet indoor dogs, while at the same time being raucous outdoor dogs.

Most of the hounds are great with children and active families, but some, like the Basset and Afghan Hound, would prefer a quieter household. These breeds cannot be left alone for long periods of time without becoming noisy and destructive. If you live in a close community and leave your hound in a kennel or crate, you'll soon be receiving calls and notes from your neighbors about your dog howling all day long.

A few of the hounds, such as the Dachshund and Basset, are able to fare well in a small home, such as a condominium or apartment, provided they receive adequate exercise. Bloodhounds and

Sporting dogs like the Weimaraner and the Vizsla need lots of exercise and socialization in order to become valued members of the family.

Because they require an assertive owner and lots of training, working dogs like the Bernese Mountain Dog are happiest with a job to do.

Irish Wolfhounds, while large, are also very quiet household dogs that do well in a home with children of all ages. However, they do need a large indoor space to accommodate their immense size. Although most hounds have easy-to-groom coats, many tend to drip saliva. Bloodhounds, in particular, can cause quite a mess when shaking their heads.

Working dogs need a job. They were bred to be watchdogs or sled dogs. Whether watching over sheep, people, or homes, or pulling a sled in the Iditarod, they perform with tireless precision. Some of these breeds might do well with children, if they are well trained and were raised with them. They adapt well to any environment, provided they receive appropriate amounts of exercise. Working dogs require assertive owners who will make sure that their dog does not become Alpha over any of the family members. Everyone in the family must discipline and work with the dog or he will not listen to their commands.

Most of the working breeds shed, drool, and require a lot of maintenance. The few short-haired breeds, like Dobermans, Boxers, Mastiffs, and Great Danes, have easy-to-care-for coats. All but the Dobermans tend to drool a lot. The longer-haired breeds, like Akitas, Bernese Mountain Dogs, Malamutes, Great Pyrenees, Newfoundlands, and Saint Bernards, require regular brushing to keep their coats in proper condition. The Schnauzer requires regular trips to a professional groomer.

The dogs bred to pull sleds, like Malamutes, Huskies, and Samoyeds, can often be difficult to train to walk with you. You will need consistency and much persistence to train these breeds. In

Most breeds have inherent talents and skills. These Alaskan Malamute puppies feel right at home doing what they were bred to do.

general, they do well in a town home or single family home, but are not recommended for an apartment or condominium unless you are willing to exercise them more than twice a day.

Most small terriers will fare well in a close community because they don't require extreme amounts of exercise as with a sporting or working breed. There are also several that are small enough to live comfortably in an apartment or condominium. They can easily learn not to be highly active indoors, provided they have something to chew on and receive appropriate amounts of outdoor exercise. Most terriers require professional grooming on a regular basis, or their coats become straggly.

Most terriers are not recommended for a home with young children. They might do well with older, considerate children provided they have been raised together. Terriers generally do best with assertive adults who will offer strict training regimens and consistency. Since most terriers were bred to hunt vermin, it is not a good idea to play games such as tug-of-war or roughhousing. They are tenacious and easily riled.

Toy breeds usually do well in any environment. They must have early socialization and training in order to be good companions. Most Toy breeds have problems with housetraining, barking, and territorial aggression, which can get very out of hand if they do not receive consistent training. Even though they are small in stature, it does not mean that they do well with small children. In fact, most are not recommended for families with active younger children because they have low tolerance for erratic behavior and are easily provoked.

The dogs in the Non-Sporting Group cannot be generalized because they are all very different. They must be addressed as individuals and your choice made accordingly.

The Bichon Frise is a friendly, outgoing little dog that requires regular trips to a professional groomer. (They do well in just about any environment whether it is a condominium or country setting.) Bichon Frises tend to have a stubborn streak, which can make housetraining difficult. However, if you work with them on a consistent basis, training should be very enjoyable.

Boston Terriers are easy to maintain and normally very outgoing. They do well with children of all ages, as long as they are considerate. Boston Terriers are easy to train but do have a tendency to bark a lot. They require a lot of exercise and adapt well to almost any environment.

Bulldogs are great companions for people with just about any lifestyle. They are amiable, easy to train, and love to play. Bulldogs don't require large amounts of exercise, but they are happy to amble along on a walk in the woods, and some even like to go swimming. Even though they have short coats, they must be meticulously maintained and their skin folds need regular cleaning. Their paws and anal areas also require maintenance. These dogs must live in a temperature-controlled environment because they are susceptible to extreme weather conditions.

Chow Chows are not dogs to be taken lightly. In fact, a Chow Chow is not a good choice for a first-time dog owner. They are highly protective of their families and not friendly with strangers. The main reason you do not want to have a Chow Chow if there are children in the house is that there are always other children coming in and out of the home that can be endangered. Chow Chows are great for someone who lives in a quiet home with few visitors. They require a owner with an assertive nature, consistent obedience training, and lots of socialization.

Dalmatians were bred to run alongside carriages all day long, which will give you a good idea of their energy level. They must have a large fenced-in area to exercise, and they must

Most terriers, like this Welsh Terrier, will get along fine with children if they are well trained and properly socialized.

Before you purchase a purebred puppy, consider the dog's original purpose and the kind of training and care he will require.

receive regular training sessions. Dalmatians live well with older, active children and are generally good with strangers, provided they received early socialization.

Keeshonden are great companions. They have very heavy coats and require regular brushing. Keeshonden adapt well to any environment, provided they receive appropriate exercise. They are easy to train, get along well with children of all ages, and have a tendency to smile when greeting their people.

Lhasa Apsos, while small enough to live comfortably in a condominium or apartment, are only recommended for homes without children or high activity levels. They are easily provoked and one should never harass them around their food or a favorite toy. Lhasa Apsos require consistent training and assertive owners.

Both the Miniature and Standard Poodles are easily trainable and love people. They do require regular trips to a professional groomer to maintain their shed-free coats. While the Miniature Poodle adjusts well to a smaller home and yard, the Standard Poodle requires lots of exercise and a large fenced-in area. They are highly active and need stimulation. When spoiled, they are sulky and can bark excessively.

Schipperkes are great with older children, but too rambunctious for young children. They are usually good with strangers but can be aggressive to unknown dogs. Although they are stubborn, they respond well to training. Some Schipperkes can become possessive of their toys and must be taught at an early age that this behavior won't be tolerated.

There are more breeds within the Non-Sporting Group than can be discussed in this book. It would be a good idea to look for books on the breed of your choice in order to get a better idea of your ideal dog.

Herding dogs, while extremely intelligent, may not be good companions in homes that have young children. These dogs will herd and chase children, bounce against them, and possibly nip at their heels. A few, such as the Old English Sheepdog and Collie, are really great with youngsters that like to hug; however, most will become very uncomfortable with being held in such a manner. Herding dogs are generally easy to train, but must receive constant stimulation. They were bred to work and can become very destructive without that outlet.

While few of the other breeds are popular, there are some worth mentioning. The American Eskimo Dog and Jack Russell Terrier have become quite popular. Neither is recommended for homes with small children and both must receive consistent training from assertive people. Early socialization is a must. They can be wonderful companions if provided with the right environment.

Even though Jack Russell Terriers are a small breed, they are highly energetic and not recommended for a condominium life. They need lots of running space. In fact, they thrive in a rural environment. The American Eskimo Dog, on the other hand, is very adaptable to most any environment, provided that he receives appropriate exercise.

A few other rare breeds growing in popularity are the Louisiana Catahoula Leopard Dog and the Shiba Inu. Both have relatively easy-to-care-for coats but can be difficult to train. They are independent, high-energy dogs that need lots of exercise. Therefore, they should only be allowed to run in a large fenced-in area, not loose. These dogs require lots of stimulation and would not do well if left alone for long periods of time.

It's easy to fall in love with an adorable puppy. Picking a purebred dog will ensure that you know as much about the puppy's background and temperament as possible.

Regardless of the breed you choose, you must consider the time required for care, exercise, and training. While most breeds are adaptable to any living condition, whether city or country, their value as a companion and working dog depends on you.

Find The Right Pup

The best place to get a quality dog is from a professional, reputable breeder. You can get referrals from a veterinarian, a friend, or by attending a dog show, which is the best method. You can access the information for the date and location of a dog show through the American Kennel Club's (AKC) website which is very informative. However, the AKC cannot recommend a breeder, but can direct you toward the breed's national club.

There are a lot of so-called purebred dogs that have been bred by puppy mills. Although there are some great dogs that come from these places, they are few and far between. Most dogs from puppy mills are of the wrong structure and/or have health problems. Worst of all, you would be supporting breeders who raise dogs in horrible living conditions, often breeding puppies as young as six months of age to close relatives. Unfortunately, most of these dogs have papers, which proves that papers can be meaningless.

Another means of obtaining a purebred dog, although you may not be able to retrieve any paperwork, are through breed rescues and animal shelters. Purebred dogs are given up as often as mixed breeds, due to having owners who are unwilling or unable to care for their needs. These organizations are often overwhelmed with purebred dogs and are looking for responsible new owners. While most of the dogs found here are older, you'll often run across puppies. However, don't dismiss an older dog. They often make the best pets. Just think...No need to worry about house-training or the destructive chewing phase. You'll already have a trustworthy dog.

You'll often run across neighbors or friends that breed dogs. Even though you may be acquainted with these people, you need to demonstrate caution when buying one of their puppies. There

Purchasing your puppy from a responsible breeder ensures that your dog will be healthy and well socialized.

are many careless breeders who do not promote the best in a breed and allow their dogs to have puppies just to make money, or maybe they want their children to see the miracle of birth. Some people breed their dog because they love that dog so much they want another of similar genetic attributes.

If you plan on having your dog around for a long time, you must be careful in your selection. Take your time and approach a quality breeder. A good breeder will have at least one of the pup's parents on the premises and will allow you to interact with him/her and show you a pedigree filled with titled dogs that aren't closely related to each other. A reputable breeder will have both parents x-rayed for hip dysplasia, have their hearts and eyes checked and have knowledge of which breeds are prone to other disorders such as von Willebrand's Disease and epilepsy, which also needs to be checked. A responsible breeder will not breed dogs that have these tendencies. Ask for certificates that prove the dog is free of any health problems.

Another plus about approaching a good breeder versus a backyard or puppy mill breeder is that you can be assured your purebred pup will meet most of the breed standards, which is important for a healthy, lifetime companion. A dog with poor conformation will most likely develop problems. For example, poorly formed hips lead to hip dysplasia. A weak heart can cause an early death. Epilepsy will increase your veterinary bills and cause you to always be anxious about your beloved dog's well-being.

A well-bred dog will also tend to have a better temperament. Most breeders take into consideration a dog's temperament as well as structure before breeding. Some will specifically breed one dog to another to complement and improve the breed line. Obtaining a dog from this type of breeder is very important; while you may just want a pet, you will be getting a very healthy, well-adjusted dog.

When looking for a quality purebred pup, avoid pet shops, neighborhood breeders, and puppy mills. Go to the dog shows, contact national breed clubs, and look in dog magazines. Dog magazines also list dog shows, which are the perfect places to find a quality breeder. When you go to a dog show, observe your favorite breeds in action. Speak to the breeders and interact with the dogs. Get the names of people who have bought dogs from a particular breeder and contact them. The best way to know if a dog will work out well in your life is to speak to others who own a dog from that particular line.

A breeder will separate their pups into two categories: show and pet quality. This allows you to make a decision based on your pup's future activities. A show-quality puppy will cost more than a pet-quality puppy. Some breeders insist on a co-ownership until the dog is titled and bred at least once, which can be troublesome for someone just wanting a pet. His or her dog will have to be shown, which means he'll be away from home for long time periods. The dog will also have the stress of either breeding and/or whelping. Unless you specifically bought the dog to show in conformation, this may not be the path to choose. This type of dog is not primarily a pet, but a showpiece.

A pet-quality dog can often participate in many other activities besides those in the breed ring, such as obedience trials, field trials, hunting, agility, and much more. The pet-quality dog may fail to meet all the AKC standards, but can still make a great companion. Obtaining a pet-quality pup from a professional breeder will ensure you get a dog that has a good temperament, is healthy, and is a decent representation of his breed. He may be a little long in the back or not the right coloring, but overall will be a beautiful animal.

Another important thing you may want to look at when approaching a professional breeder is how the puppies were raised. A pup that has only lived in a kennel has not learned about the world and will tend to be timid and unsociable. Look for signs that the pups have been home-raised, such as if they are comfortable in most situations. Home-raised puppies receive lots of attention and are exposed to noises and movements that a kennel pup never experiences.

Another way to ensure that you obtain a healthy puppy is to inspect the kennel area, which should be clean and have plenty of fresh air and water accessible to the pup. Also, the puppies should be clean and free of fleas and lacerations.

Diligent breeders begin teaching the puppies where to go potty as early as five weeks of age. A large area filled with sand or wood chips easily accessible to the pups works nicely. Most dogs choose to potty outside their dens, and providing an area with an absorbent surface aids in the overall housetraining process.

Even if the puppy you choose is not of show quality, he can still make a loving pet.

By breeding only the healthiest dogs, the breeder ensures the long life and good temperament of each puppy.

Breeders should begin handling the pups well before they open their eyes. They should be touched all over, spoken to, and manipulated. Background sounds such as music, city noises, and dog show noises all condition the puppies to accept any new environment. A well-bred puppy will welcome your touch.

A reputable breeder will offer the utmost care to both the mother and the resulting puppies and will screen his or her dogs for genetic diseases before breeding them.

Before taking your puppy home, the breeder should hand you a packet that holds the puppy's registration papers, pedigree, and medical history. Most pups receive their first worming at five weeks of age and another at seven weeks. They should also have their first inoculations by the age of seven weeks.

The best time to bring home your new purebred puppy is between the ages of seven to ten weeks. Some breeders will hold their dogs until 12 weeks, which is rare. From the age of seven weeks, puppies begin their permanent bonding with their pack. This pup will come to you with a clean slate, open to learn and clear of behavior problems. You can mold him to your life.

Choose Wisely

Now that you have an idea of which breed you want, you'll need to decide which individual puppy will best suit you and your lifestyle. Do you want a male or female? A bold or quiet pup? A pup with a strong drive or one that just likes to cuddle?

There are some major things to consider when choosing between a male and female dog. First, most male dogs tend to be more independent and prone to wandering. They want to control their packs and may be more easily provoked into aggression. Male dogs are often harder to walk with, because they want to stop at every mailbox and fire hydrant to leave their scent mark. Due to their inborn need to patrol their territory, male dogs can often be more difficult to housetrain. Unless trained very early, a male dog can prove challenging.

Female dogs are generally more amiable and easier to train than male dogs. They rarely want to control their people, although they often try to control the other animals in the household. Female dogs are easier to walk with and have less of a tendency toward aggression and dominance. They rarely react to strange dogs aggressively. While there are many exceptions to these examples, one can still generalize these attributes.

The decision on whether you want a bold or submissive puppy rests solely on your personality. A puppy that is climbing all over you and biting your feet can reasonably be considered bold. If you have children in your home, a bold puppy may not be the best idea. Think about the pup as he gets older and develops stronger jaw power. A child can be hurt from a pup that believes he's in charge. If you are an assertive adult that lives alone or with another assertive adult, a bold puppy can work out fine.

A very submissive puppy also may not be the best choice to have around children. This type of pup should be with adults in a quiet home. An outgoing puppy who easily submits and eagerly follows people may be the best type of dog to own if you have a family and also want to pursue a dog sport, such as obedience trials, agility, or field work.

The temperament of the puppy you choose will be a deciding factor in how he gets along with all your family members, especially children.

The Puppy Aptitude Temperament test, or (PAT), developed by Wendy Volhard, as published in the AKC Gazette will guide you in the right direction. This test first enlightens you on what kind of companion your puppy will be, and then helps detect specific abilities for future activities.

The PAT should be done in a quiet area that is free of all distractions. The tester should be knowledgeable in the procedures, but also be someone that the puppy doesn't already know. A good breeder will test his puppies every so often to make sure they go into the right homes, but this is still not a completely accurate means of predicting a pup's future personality. Most puppies will automatically cling to someone they know and easily submit to a person who has never allowed misbehavior.

Test 1: Social Attraction

This test is utilized to discover the degree of social attraction, dependence, and confidence. The pup is put in the quiet area and the tester tries to coax him away from the entrance by gently clapping her hands and kneeling down.

Scoring
1. The dog came readily, tail up, jumped and bit at the tester's hands.
2. The dog came readily, tail up, pawed, and licked tester's hands.
3. The dog came readily, tail up.
4. The dog came readily, tail down.
5. The dog came with hesitation, tail down.
6. The dog didn't come at all.

Test 2: Following

The purpose of this test is to see how dependent the pup is on people. The tester stands up and walks away from the pup in a normal manner. The response is then noted as follows:

Scoring
1. The dog followed readily, tail up, bit at the feet, and generally tangled in the legs.
2. The dog followed readily, tail up, and bit at tester's feet.
3. The dog followed readily, tail up.
4. The dog followed with hesitation, tail down.
5. The dog watched tester walk away and did not follow.
6. The dog went in different direction.

Test 3: Restraint

The restraint test will expose the pup's degree of dominance or submission when socially/physically dominated. The tester crouches down and gently rolls the pup onto his back, holding him with one hand for up to 30 seconds.

Scoring

1. The dog struggled fiercely and bit.
2. The dog struggled fiercely and flailed.
3. The dog settled, struggled, settled with some eye contact.
4. The dog struggled, then settled.
5. The dog did not struggle.
6. The dog did not struggle, but strained to avoid eye contact.

Test 4: Social Dominance

Test 4 will expose the puppy's degree of accepting dominance from others. The tester allows the puppy to stand up while he is being stroked from his head down toward his back. The stroking continues until a recognizable behavior, such as trying to move away or crouching down occurs.

Scoring

1. The dog jumped, pawed, and bit.
2. The dog jumped and pawed.
3. The dog cuddled up to tester and tried to lick her face.
4. The dog squirmed and licked at tester's hands.
5. The dog rolled over and licked tester's hands.
6. The dog went away and stayed away.

Watching how your pup plays with his littermates will tell you a lot about his personality.

Test 5: Elevation Dominance

This demonstrates how much manipulation the puppy accepts while in a position of no control. The tester bends over and cradles the puppy under his belly intertwining her fingers, with the palms up. The tester then elevates the puppy a short distance off the ground for approximately 30 seconds.

Scoring

1. The dog struggled fiercely and bit.
2. The dog struggled fiercely.
3. The dog did not struggle, just relaxed.
4. The dog struggled, then settled, and licked.
5. The dog did not struggle, licked at hands.
6. The dog did not struggle, just froze.

In these five tests, you are able to discover your puppy's future behavioral tendencies or the kind of companion he will be. A bold puppy has scores that range from 1's to 3's. Keep in mind, however, that a pup scoring mostly 1's will be extremely dominant and difficult to train. A puppy that will be good with children, easy to train, and very social, will score 3's and 4's. A very submissive and quiet pup scores 5's and 6's. This pup needs a quiet home with a regular schedule and low activity. He might do well with the elderly or a home without children. This type of puppy will also prove to be fearful and unsociable and not a real cuddlesome pup.

Test 6: Retrieving

This exercise exposes the pup's natural degree of willingness to work with people and his ability to do many different types of activities, from obedience trials and fieldwork to agility and search and rescue. The tester crouches beside the puppy and attracts his attention with a crumpled-up paper ball. When the puppy shows interest by looking at the ball, the tester tosses the object four to six feet in front of the pup.

Scoring

1. The dog chases the object, picks it up, and runs away to play with it.
2. The dog chases the object and stands over it, but does not return.
3. The dog chases the object and returns with the object to the tester.
4. The dog chases the object and returns to the tester without it.
5. The dog starts to chase the object but quickly loses interest.
6. The dog does not show interest at all.

Test 7: Touch Sensitivity

This will let you know how sensitive your pup might be to rough hands or young children's erratic movements. It is also a great way to discover if your pup might make a good therapy dog. The tester takes hold of the webbing between your puppy's toes and gently presses the tender flesh between her forefinger and thumb. The pressure gets firmer and firmer until the pup reacts by pulling away or otherwise showing discomfort.

Scoring

1. The dog waits eight to ten counts before responding.
2. The dog waits six to seven counts before responding.
3. The dog waits five to six counts before responding.
4. The dog waits two to four counts before responding.
5. The dog waits one to two counts before responding.
6. The dog cringes from the touch entirely.

Test 8: Sound Sensitivity

Not only is this a great test for a future guard dog, but also helps you discover whether a puppy might have difficulty hearing. The puppy is placed in the center of the testing area. The tester or an assistant makes a sharp noise a few feet from the puppy. This can be a book dropping, keys rattling, a metal spoon striking sharply on a metal pan, or the tooting of a horn.

Scoring

1. The dog listens, locates the sound, walks toward it, and barks.
2. The dog listens, locates the sound, and barks.
3. The dog listens, locates the sound, shows curiosity, and walks toward it.
4. The dog listens and locates the sound, but remains in place.
5. The dog cringes, backs off, and hides.
6. The dog ignores the sound.

Test 9: Sight Sensitivity

This test demonstrates your dog's degree of response to new things. Is he curious or afraid? The tester puts the pup in the center of the test area. Using a string attached to a towel, the tester jerks the towel across the floor a few feet away from the puppy.

Scoring:

1. The dog looks at the towel, attacks, and bites at it.
2. The dog looks at the towel and barks at it with his tail held up.
3. The dog looks at the towel and attempts to investigate.
4. The dog looks, barks, and tucks his tail.
5. The dog has no response.
6. The dog runs away and hides.

A well-socialized puppy will accept gentle handling and petting and will thrive in any environment.

A puppy that has scored mostly 1's and 2's in tests 6 through 9 is extremely dominant and will be difficult to include in future dog sports, unless he is worked with consistently by an assertive owner. He may be quick to bite and is not a dog to have around children or elderly residents. When this dog also shows a 1 or 2 score in the touch sensitivity test, he might be difficult to train.

If the dog scores mostly 2's, he may respond well to firm and fair handling by an assertive adult, although he will test his parameters from time to time. He will, however, have a bouncy, outgoing personality but be too active for a home with young children or elderly residents.

A puppy that scores mostly 3's is one that easily accepts humans as leaders and companions. He is the best prospect for a novice owner and adapts well to new situations. He'll probably thrive in a home with children, but may be too rambunctious for elderly residents. This type of dog will be a good prospect for dog sports and activities. This puppy will be curious and easily adapt to most situations.

A pup that scores mostly 4's will be submissive and work well in most households. He may be slightly less outgoing and reserved, but will get along well with quiet children and elderly residents. He'll be easy to train and may do well in some dog sports such as obedience trials and fieldwork.

Should your dog score mostly 5's, he'll be extremely submissive and will require gentle, patient handling during training. He will need to have his confidence built through gradual exposure and must have a structured environment. This type of dog will not work well with a novice dog owner, because he is easily frightened. He may work well in a home with older adults that live a quiet lifestyle.

A dog with mostly 6's is extremely independent and may not be affectionate. Most puppies do not fall into this category unless they've had bad experiences. This pup is not a good prospect for a home with children or high activity. He is also not a good working prospect. His person must be patient, reserved, and understand that he is easily frightened.

If the tester sees no clear pattern throughout the tests, the puppy may not be feeling well. He may have been recently wormed or inoculated. It would be a good idea to wait a few days and retest. In fact, it is always a good idea to do the PAT test at least twice; once at five weeks of age and the second time at seven weeks of age.

If you have a specific activity in mind such as flyball, Frisbee™, or obedience work, you'll want to add a few things to the tests. One is watching your potential pup's reaction to different objects, such as a tennis ball, disc, or bone. Does he want to fetch all of them or just one in particular? If you want a dog for search and rescue work, you can try hiding a toy where the pup can easily locate it. Each time you hide the toy, make the retrieval of it more difficult. For example, the first time you place it in plain sight. The second time you place it in an area hidden by a chair or board. The third time, hide it entirely, and your dog's dedication to locating the toy will show you how adept a search and rescue dog he might become.

Pick the puppy that picks you! The pup you choose should be bright-eyed, healthy looking, and eager to be with you.

Had you obtained your new purebred puppy with the intention of having a therapy dog, you'll want the cuddliest, quietest one you can find. He won't need to have retrieving abilities, although that is a plus. Simon must be calm and accepting, not overly sensitive. He should allow your children to play dress up with him and enjoy going places with you and others.

Make sure you choose your puppy according to your living conditions, family members, and plans for the future. Simon is to be an integral part of your family and must fit in. This is a choice for life, not a life to throw away.

Some puppies may have a submissive personality and will require gentle handling and a patient owner in order to live up to their potential.

Puppy Care

A purebred puppy has to have the proper nutrition, grooming, veterinary care, and attention. In order to develop into a healthy, happy dog, he must also have plenty of mental stimulation. While caring for a puppy means paying attention to his nutritional, veterinary, and grooming needs, it also means that you must help build his confidence through socialization and experience. He must have a means of occupying his time. Puppies cannot read books or play with dolls, although many would happily chew on these things. Young puppies spend their time chewing, digging, and romping. It's up to you to keep them occupied in a constructive manner.

Let's first take a look at your purebred puppy's nutrition. While nursing from his mother, Simon received all the nutrients he needed to remain healthy. By the time Simon reached four weeks of age, his mother began to wean him and teach him how to eat solid food. At the time of weaning, breeders begin feeding their puppies food that is high in fat and protein to make sure that they can maintain their fast growth and high energy levels.

Due to Simon's small stomach and high activity level, he should be fed three to four times per day. His metabolism works quickly, sending the food through almost as fast as he eats it. Keep this in mind when working on housetraining, because Simon will have to potty within 10 to 15 minutes after eating. Because of his small teeth, moisten your pup's food with warm water or a bit of milk, which aids his digestion process, partially breaking down the food before it reaches his stomach.

Having researched what works best for their type of dog, many breeders have preferred food brands. Unless Simon is having digestion problems or the food is of low quality, stick to whatever brand he was eating prior to going home with you. If you have no idea what he was getting, ask your veterinarian and check the labels on his puppy food. A good protein level is between 33 and 43 percent. The fat content should also be high—over 8 percent. These high levels of protein and fat are necessary for normal growth and the production of antibodies to aid in a pup's overall ability to fight infection and heal quickly.

A pup with a super sensitive digestive system would do well on a chicken- or lamb-based meal. Check for fillers, such as plant source ingredients and ground by-products by reading the first three ingredients on the bag. If it says corn meal or bone meal, you should try another brand. Dogs don't spend their time munching in cornfields, nor do they eat only powdered bones. While grains, like rice and barley, and vegetables help maintain overall vitamin balance, puppies need muscle meat. They get most of their protein through meats such as chicken, fish, turkey, beef, eggs, and dairy products.

While you may be tempted to spoil Simon by offering him table scraps or feeding him by hand, don't fall into this trap. Dogs need the nutrients from their dog food and, most of all, they need to learn to eat out of their own dishes. Be sure to feed Simon at the same place and approximately the same time each day. Don't worry if he doesn't finish every meal. Hand feeding him the remainder will only turn into a bad habit. Simon will come to expect this and may turn up his nose at his dog food.

Most young puppies have a tendency to eat just about anything. Like human babies, puppies are very orally inclined. While you're walking Simon, he'll eat mulch, dirt, leaves, dropped candy wrappers, and cigarette butts. This will often lead to gastrointestinal upset, which in turn will make

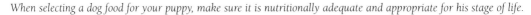

When selecting a dog food for your puppy, make sure it is nutritionally adequate and appropriate for his stage of life.

him vomit or have diarrhea. Keep a constant watch on where Simon's little nose travels and take anything from his mouth that isn't an edible object. If you notice gastrointestinal distress, take your puppy's stool sample to the veterinarian. A mild case of gastritis is easily treated by feeding a bland diet for a few days, such as boiled chicken, cottage cheese, and rice. Once your puppy is feeling better, gradually, over the course of several days, return him to his normal food. A brief fast never hurts. In fact, wild canines will often fast if they don't feel well or if they spent a day gorging.

Periodically check Simon's weight. He'll be growing like a weed, but during the first four months he should still appear well-rounded. Run your hand along his sides and feel for his ribs. You should barely be able to feel the individual ribs. There should also be a slight indent at his waist and you should not be able to clearly feel or see his hip bones.

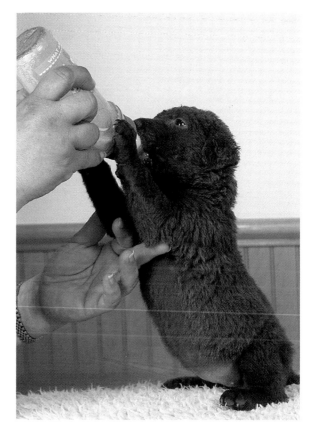

A newborn puppy will receive all the nutrition he requires from nursing; however, once he is weaned, he will depend on you to fulfill his needs.

As Simon ages, he'll need to be fed more and will be able to hold more food at one time. You'll find that he might wean himself off his noon meal, which normally occurs at four to five months of age. At this time, you can reduce his feeding times to twice a day. While Simon grows, offer him as much as he'll eat, provided you don't see him becoming overweight. When he reaches six months of age, through the course of a week, gradually wean him off his puppy food and switch to an adult maintenance diet. This will help prevent growing pains, which is a common occurrence in fast growing, large dogs. Supplementing his diet with Vitamins C and E will also help his growing bones and muscles. Adding a bit of Brewer's Yeast and garlic will help repel parasites while also maintaining his digestive health.

Although your pup may not have long hair now, he still needs to learn about being groomed. If you acquired your puppy at a kennel, he may be in need of a bath first thing. Plus, puppies like to roll in the stinkiest things they can find, which comes from their instinctive hunting drives of trying to camouflage their scent so their prey cannot smell them in the vicinity. Have you thought about how you're going to bathe your pup?

The best place to bathe Simon for the first time would be in the kitchen or laundry room sink or, if he is too large for these containers, the bathtub. The bottom of the sink or tub should have a

Provide your puppy with cool, clean water at all times.

nonslip surface, which can be achieved with a rubber mat or by placing a towel on the bottom of the area before filling the tub with warm water.

Have all your bathing supplies ready: puppy shampoo, a dry towel, a floating toy, and treats. It would also be a good idea to stick cotton balls in his ears to prevent moisture from entering the ear canal. If you wish to wash his face, put a bland ophthalmic ointment in his eyes to prevent irritation from the shampoo.

You'll want to make Simon's first bath a positive experience. This won't be a problem for some breeds of dog, such as retrievers and spaniels. However, others will still shake and pout no matter what you do. While you bathe Simon, give him lots of praise and a treat now and then. You can float a toy in the water, such as a squeaky rubber duck, which will make for a fun and positive experience.

If you intend for Simon to be a housedog, as all dogs should be, then you will need to bathe him every ten days to two weeks. This will keep him from getting a doggy odor and make him more pleasant to hug. Regular bathing also maintains his coat, reducing shedding and dander.

Always make sure that you thoroughly dry Simon after his bath, and never let him go outside while still wet. Puppies can easily catch a chill, which lowers their resistance to airborne bacteria and viruses. Rub him vigorously with a towel until he is mostly dry.

Establish a brushing routine. Not only does brushing help you notice any abnormalities, it also helps with bonding. Brushing regularly removes loose hair, eliminates tangles, and distributes skin oil. A long-haired dog will need brushing every day, so if Simon will eventually have long hair, then begin the brushing routine from day one. A short-haired breed will require brushing only one or two days per week, but it doesn't hurt to give a quick once over whenever your puppy is exposed to an environment that might harbor parasites, such as the woods, tall grass, or an area with shrubs.

The type of brush you use will depend on your dog's coat. With a pup however, stick to a soft bristle brush to make sure grooming remains a positive experience. Begin first by brushing the head and ears. Then do Simon's chest, front legs, back, sides, tummy, and hindquarters. Finish by doing his tail. Brush gently but firmly enough to make sure all the loose hair and dander is removed. A grooming glove would be ideal, because it allows you to pet your dog clean.

Simon's toenails will need attention every six to eight weeks. Puppy nails are very sharp and can easily shred fabric or cut your skin. It's a good idea to get Simon used to this process as early as possible, because he needs to remain absolutely still while this is done. At first, you might want to get someone to help you hold him while you trim the nails. This will ensure you don't trim too closely. Cutting into the pink pulpy part of his nail will cause severe bleeding as well as give Simon a bad experience.

Look closely at the nail. It will appear similar in shape to a hawk's beak. The best place to trim is a quarter inch before the sharp hook. Above this hook will be the pulpy part of the nail, similar to the pink part of your own nails. Below this is the clear part of the nail, the safe place to trim. If Simon has black nails, which make it difficult to see the separation, trim off a little at a time until

you are close to where the nail hooks. If you are at all squeamish about this procedure, try trimming off just the very end and then filing it a little further. An electric clipper works very well and saves lots of time.

Ear cleaning is also required for Simon's overall health, especially if your pup is the type with floppy ears. Floppy ears don't allow good air circulation to dry out excess moisture. Trapped moisture can cause ear infections. Some infections are caused by mites while others are from yeast and dirt build up. A weekly cleaning will ensure Simon's ears remain in top condition. The last thing you want to deal with are ear infections, which can not only cause your pup much discomfort, but can also eventually make him go deaf from repeated damage to his middle ear.

An ear infection is pretty easy to recognize. The pup will be shaking his head a lot or rubbing his head on furniture, and

Regular grooming will not only keep your puppy looking good, it will also help you to keep on top of any health problems he may experience.

you will detect an unpleasant odor in his ears. If this occurs, take Simon to your veterinarian immediately for treatment.

There are many ear-cleaning products on the market, however, you can also use mineral oil. Place a bit of the fluid on a soft rag, and gently clean Simon's outer ear, taking special care around the features. To clean a little deeper, put some fluid on a cotton swab. Do *not* go into the ear canal. Keep all your attention on the outer ear only. Your veterinarian is the only one who should clean Simon's inner ear. Repeated assault on the inner ear canal can damage your pup's eardrum.

Some dogs have a lot of hair in their ears. You may not see much of this until Simon reaches adolescence. The fine hairs can disrupt air flow, trapping dirt and moisture. Take a pair of tweezers and pull out only the hairs that come out easily. Don't pull stubborn hairs. This will make Simon cry out and remind him of how painful the experience can be. Remember, you want to keep everything as positive as possible. If Simon is extremely sensitive on all the hairs in his ears, use a small pair of scissors and trim the hairs off. You should only do this, however, if Simon will sit very still for you.

Regular eye cleaning will also be important for dogs with protruding eyes, such as Pomeranians, Boston Terriers, Chihuahuas, and Lhasa Apsos. It would also be a good idea to regularly clean the eyes of dogs that have long facial hair. Redness or a discharge could mean either an irritation or infection. A saline otic solution can be used once a week to keep them clear. Always check for dirt particles and hair in the eyes. Trimming the hair around Simon's eyes will be helpful in keeping the eyes clear. As he grows, get your dog accustomed to wearing long hair in a barrette or bow on his forehead. Allowing your dog to live with hair constantly over his eyes can eventually make him nearsighted.

Your puppy's feet must be inspected regularly and his toenails kept trimmed to prevent any injuries.

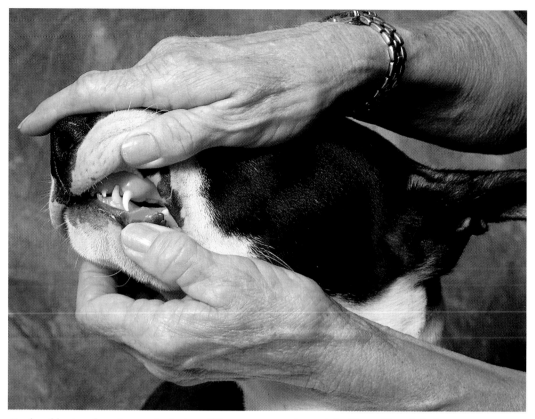

Good oral hygiene from the very beginning will keep your puppy's mouth healthy and breath fresh.

Something most puppy owners ignore is dental hygiene. Feeding hard biscuits or dry food is not sufficient to clean the teeth. While biscuits do help reduce tartar buildup, they do not effectively rid the teeth of plaque and tartar. Simon's gums will need special attention from the start to prevent periodontal disease. This is especially important if you have a Toy breed. These dogs tend to have more dental problems than other breeds.

Even while Simon has his baby teeth, you should begin brushing at least twice per week. Granted, his baby teeth do fall out, but it is the process that you are getting him acclimated to, not just the matter of keeping his teeth clean and breath fresh.

Regular brushing will avoid those yearly trips to the veterinarian to have Simon's teeth scaled. It will also help prolong his life in many ways. First, he will keep his teeth longer enabling him to properly chew his food. Secondly, it will prevent periodontal disease, an infection of the gums. Periodontal disease not only causes his teeth to fall out but also transfers bacteria to his organs, reducing their efficacy. While you may not see these problems while Simon is a pup, they will arise later, so it's a good idea to begin the process early.

You can use a child's toothbrush, a finger brush that is specially manufactured for cleaning canine teeth, or even a soft rag. Put some doggy toothpaste on the surface of your implement and clean each tooth in a circular motion, including the gums around the tooth. Simon may give you the most problems in cleaning his lower teeth. Be patient and aim for one at a time. Allow him a breather every so often.

Your veterinarian will put your puppy on a vaccination schedule to prevent him from contracting certain life-threatening diseases.

You should take your new purebred puppy to see the veterinarian within the first few days of ownership. He needs to receive a complete physical, be checked for parasites, and begin his vaccination routines. The first inoculation should be when Simon is six weeks of age. This is followed by a series of boosters, the rabies vaccine, and a kennel cough inhalant. By the time Simon is six months old, he'll have everything he needs to fight the most common canine infections. With yearly boosters, he'll maintain immunity.

Simon's first shot will be a combination vaccine, called an all-in-one. This is the preferred method, which involves only one shot, instead of five, to deliver the medication. This all-in-one inoculation includes parvovirus, leptospirosis, hepatitis, parainfluenza, and canine distemper.

Parvovirus is a disease that attacks the intestinal tract, white blood cells, and heart muscles. Young puppies are very susceptible to airborne contagions and can respond violently to parvovirus through heart failure. The symptoms include diarrhea, vomiting, not eating, and a high fever, and if left untreated it can be fatal.

Leptospirosis is a bacterial disease that is transmitted either by contact with the urine or objects contaminated by the urine of an infected dog. This disease can result in kidney failure.

Hepatitis attacks a pup's liver. Sometimes a puppy can get a respiratory infection as a secondary symptom. As with leptospirosis, hepatitis results in contact with the urine or objects touched by the urine of an infected animal. Once there is liver damage, scarring occurs which reduces the liver's ability to function properly.

Parainfluenza is not as fatal as the previously described diseases, but can cause much discomfort, nevertheless. Should your pup have contact with the nasal secretions of a dog with this virus, he can show symptoms of upper respiratory distress, such as sneezing, nasal discharge, and overall lethargy.

Canine distemper is not only spread through contact with the nasal secretions of infected dogs, but also through contact with ocular secretions. This virus can also be carried on air currents or inanimate objects. First, the affected pup would show respiratory distress and flu-like symptoms. If not treated in time, distemper can be fatal.

If you plan on attending a group training class or boarding Simon in a kennel at any time, you should request that he receive the bordetella vaccine. This vaccine is usually dispatched through a nasal spray. The bordetella vaccine guards against two strains of kennel cough, which are highly contagious airborne diseases. The symptoms include coughing and nasal secretions. Without treatment, it can blossom into a worse problem, such as bronchitis.

There are two other vaccines that you should request. One is Lyme disease vaccine and the other is a coronavirus vaccine. Lyme disease is transmitted through tick bites. If you live in an area where ticks are prevalent, make sure Simon has this yearly inoculation. Lyme disease creeps into your pup's system first causing achy muscles and lethargy. Eventually, it can cause complete paralysis and death.

Although maternal antibodies protect your puppy from disease the first few weeks of life, vaccinations are needed because they are only temporarily effective.

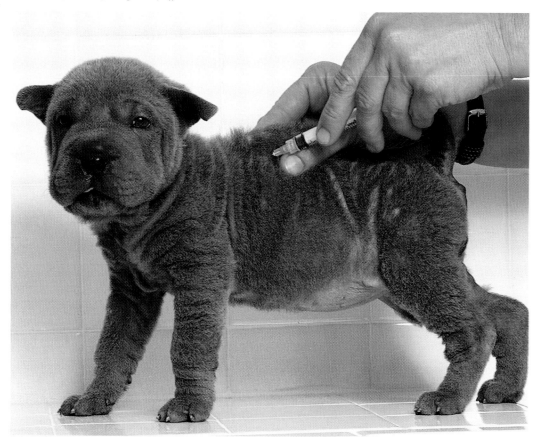

Puppies love to chew, so provide your puppy with lots of safe chew toys to keep his teeth healthy.

Coronavirus is usually a mild infection; however, young puppies and old dogs are very susceptible. The symptoms include diarrhea, vomiting, and fever. Coronavirus is similar in many ways to parvovirus, only not as severe. Caught early, your pup will make a complete recovery.

If you have a puppy that enjoys swimming, there is a new vaccine on the market to protect against giardia. Unfortunately, our waterways are polluted with waste and contaminates. Once ingested, a pup can contract the giardia bacteria which causes loose, mucousy stools. The only means of detecting this bacteria is from a stool sample taken directly from the rectum of the puppy. The bacteria dies quickly when outside of the canine system so taking a stool sample to your veterinarian will not detect it.

Simon can't tell you how he's feeling so you'll have no way of knowing if he's infected until you see the symptoms. By the time symptoms appear, the damage might already have been done, so make sure you cover all your bases.

The all-important rabies vaccine is given when Simon reaches three months of age and then again a year later. After the first year, the rabies vaccine won't have to be repeated until three to five years later, depending on the type used. However, all other vaccines will need to be repeated yearly.

Ask your veterinarian to begin Simon on a parasite control regimen including heartworm preventative and flea control. There are many different products currently on the market to aid in this most worthy of causes. Heartworm infestation is a very serious problem and, if not caught in time, can prove fatal. You can begin Simon on a preventative path as young as eight weeks of age. There are several different types of chewable tablets available. Some medications offer heartworm, hookworm, and whipworm preventatives, as well as a flea control.

If you are already dealing with a flea infestation, or regularly take Simon to places where fleas are present, you'll want to use a topical solution to both repel and kill fleas. Many products are applied directly onto the skin between Simon's shoulder blades and are specially formulated to not harm a young pup's tender skin. As Simon grows, you can switch to a product that offers coverage against ticks, as well as fleas and mosquitoes.

Mental stimulation in the form of toys, games, and training is of the utmost importance. Keeping Simon busy will curb him from becoming destructive. Offer him several different types of toys. Let

Simon have only large bones. When the bones become small or if he tears off a small chunk, throw it away. Little pieces of flat rawhide or rawhide sticks can easily lodge in the roof of his mouth or throat, causing him to choke. Also, rawhide is not digestible. If Simon receives a lot of rawhide, he can vomit or have diarrhea. Keep the rawhide bone as a special once-in-a-while treat. The people who make Nylabones™ also make Boodavelvets™. The Boodavelvet™ is a completely edible and digestible hard bone made of cornstarch or vegetables. Simon will enjoy a Boodavelvet™ as much as he would a rawhide bone. You can also offer rubber toys and Gumabone™. Regardless of the toy, Simon will be more enthusiastic about it if you play with him.

Rotate Simon's toys daily to maintain his interest in them. Present him with three toys one day and a different three the next so each time his reaction will be, "Oh boy! A new toy!"

The best way to keep Simon stimulated is to train and teach him tricks. Puppies love learning, especially if it involves getting special rewards and praise. Don't wait until Simon is six months old—start now. Puppies as young as eight weeks are ready and able to comprehend and respond to commands. In fact, you're essentially starting with an open mind that is searching for direction. Waiting too long will mean correcting behavioral problems and facing a resistant adolescent who feels he should be in charge. Begin Simon on the right track, and he'll never let you down.

Proper Behavior

You have gone through the process of selecting just the right purebred pup. Now you need to make sure you turn him into the perfect companion, which does not happen automatically. Puppies are not born knowing where to go potty, what to chew on, and how to get attention. They feel things out on a trial and error basis. Simon's mother taught him how to control his behavior toward her. Now you need to take up where she left off and teach him how to behave in your home.

Puppies can handle learning many new things at the same time. Putting off a lesson only makes it more difficult to correct in the future. From day one, you are setting precedents. Be consistent no matter what the situation, and Simon will learn quickly.

Crate Training and Housetraining

Housetraining success depends on the following: containment, setting a schedule, praising when Simon does the right thing, and supervising constantly. Having a place to contain Simon will make the entire process much easier. You will need a crate or pen that is not much larger than your puppy. If you wish to get a crate that will fit Simon when he is full-grown, use cinder blocks or a crate divider to make the crate temporarily smaller. He should have just enough space to turn a circle, stand, and lay down. Any more room and he'll be apt to potty on one side.

Whenever you cannot spend time with Simon, he is to be in the crate. Simon will easily accept crate training, because it simulates a den where a mother dog gives birth and raises her young. In the wild, puppies are taught by their mothers to go potty outside their den. With these instincts already in place, Simon will learn to contain himself while in his crate. The only

Crate training is the quickest and easiest way to housetrain your puppy.

time that crate training may be confusing for a puppy is if he has been left in a crate for a long period of time without the chance to relieve himself outdoors. This is commonly seen in puppies from pet shops and puppy mills.

Crate training is very easy and should never be forced. Place Simon's toys, bed, and water in the crate. Feeding him in his crate will immediately give Simon positive associations and he will quickly settle in. Allow Simon to have access to his crate when he roams freely. He needs a room to call his own just in case he gets tired or anxious about his surroundings.

If you have to leave Simon by himself for long hours every day, do not leave him in his crate. This is not humane and it may take longer to housetrain him, but there are ways to both make him feel less confined and to facilitate proper potty associations. If you must leave for long hours, place Simon's crate inside a pen, such as an exercise pen or larger chain-link pen. You still don't want to give him lots of area; just enough so he can stretch his legs and move around a bit. The surface should be easy to clean, such as linoleum, concrete, or tile. Obtain either a small child's pool or metal tray with low sides and place it on the side of the pen opposite his crate, water, and bed. Fill the container with dirt, wood chips, or sod to simulate the outdoors. Simon will most likely potty there, since dogs prefer to do their business on an absorbent surface.

Puppies kept in crates and never let out during the formative ages of four to twelve weeks may be more difficult to housetrain, but it can still be accomplished through proper feeding and scheduling. You may have to take the bed out of the crate for a short period of time, because as long as there's something to soak up the urine, the pup may continue to wet on it.

Setting a schedule is one of the most important aspects of making sure Simon learns quickly. You'll need to schedule his relief times to coincide with his feeding, play, and nap times. You can be assured that every puppy will have to go potty within ten minutes after eating (this time elongates as the puppy ages), directly upon waking from a nap, and shortly after playing.

Knowing these times will make it easier to take Simon to his relief area before an accident occurs. Consistency with these elements will ensure quick success and fewer spots on the carpet. It will also make for a more positive relationship between you and your puppy.

Here's a sample schedule to get you started:

6:00 a.m.—Take Simon outside as soon as you wake up.

6:15 a.m.—Feed Simon.

6:25 a.m.—Take Simon outside.

7:00 a.m.-11:00 a.m.—Take Simon outside every hour to go potty.

This will need to be continued until Simon reaches three months. At this time you can begin to elongate the intervals between relief times, gradually working up to four hours by the time Simon is six months old. Many dogs can hold it for much longer than four hours, but it is not fair to make them do so. Put yourself in their place and see if you could contain yourself for 12 hours every day. Most people have to relieve themselves every four hours, so it is only fair to allow Simon the same opportunity. Making a dog hold his waste for long periods of time can damage his digestive system.

12 noon—Feed Simon.

12:15 p.m.—Take Simon outside to go potty.

1:00 p.m.-3 p.m.—Continue to take Simon outside every hour or directly after a nap or play period.

4 p.m.—Feed Simon.

4:15 p.m.—Take Simon outside.

5:00 p.m.-10:00 p.m.—Take him outside every hour, especially if you are playing with him. Don't give Simon any food after his 4 p.m. meal, and take away his water around 8 p.m.

11 p.m.—Take Simon outside for his last potty of the day. Make sure Simon does something before putting him to bed in his crate. Put an ice cube in his water dish. This will keep him hydrated through the night, plus it's a great treat.

Sometimes puppies become distracted by the outdoors that they forget why they are outside. You're standing there waiting and waiting and all Simon's doing is smelling the clover. This can become very tiresome, so instead of allowing Simon to become distracted, return him to his crate and try again a half hour later. The last thing you need is to have to wait outside while Simon wanders around sniffing. This can be especially frustrating in bad weather. Your puppy must learn that the reason he has been taken outside was primarily for relieving himself. Once he has done so, he can then play and explore.

One of the ways to make housetraining even easier is to teach Simon to go potty on command. This will save you long hours of waiting for him to do his business. Begin by taking him outside as soon as he wakes up in the morning. He'll most definitely have to go potty. Say a single word over and over, such as "Hurry," "Potty,"

Your puppy will have to eliminate after sleeping, eating, and playing, so be sure to take him outside several times a day.

"Business," etc. As soon as Simon goes, praise him and give him a treat. Every time you take him outside, say the potty word until he performs. Always praise him and make a fuss when he responds. Puppies become very excited when they begin connecting your words with their actions. Within a few days, Simon will be going potty on command.

Always keep an eye on Simon while he's outside of his crate or pen. There are telltale signs of when he needs to go potty. First, if you always take him out the same door to his relief area, he'll most likely head in that direction. Second, should he not be in the vicinity of the door, he'll circle and sniff. Another possible cue is when he sits and stares at you. Many puppies that know where they must go potty will stare at their owner and try to use telepathic vibrations to get the message across. Obviously, this rarely works, so if you see any of these behaviors, get your dog outside or there is sure to be an accident. It is a far more positive training practice to avoid accidents and punishment through consistency and observation.

If you practice these procedures and Simon still has accidents, try teaching your puppy to tell you when he needs to go outside. Since he can't stand up and say, "I've gotta go now," we need to communicate in a more universal manner. Teach Simon to ring a bell to let you know.

Hang a large bell on the doorknob of the door Simon passes through to go to his relief area. The bell needs to hang low enough for him to make it move. Each time before you take him outside, rub a little cheese on the bell and show it to Simon. When he licks the cheese, the

Praise your pup profusely when he eliminates in the proper place.

bell will make noise. As soon as you hear the bell ring, quickly take him outside to his relief area and give a potty command. As soon as he finishes going potty, give him a treat. Wow! Simon just got double reinforcement for doing the right thing. If you have the time and the weather is cooperative, allow your puppy to remain outside for a while. There is much to explore in the sights and smells of the world. Dogs thrive on discovering new odors.

In a week or less, Simon will go directly to the door, ring the bell, and you will have a housetrained dog. Not only that, your friends will be very impressed.

Preventing Bad Habits

An ounce of prevention is worth a pound of cure, or so the old tale goes. This is especially true in the case of raising a puppy. Prevent the problem so you don't have to cure it later.

When crate training your puppy, provide him with a soft blanket and lots of toys. He will soon consider the crate his home away from home.

Young puppies have not yet established bad habits. The best way to ensure Simon doesn't become destructive is to never allow it in the first place. While you may think, "Oh, he's just a puppy. He'll get over it," this is not the case. Whatever you allow him to do as a pup, he will also do as an adult dog. A young puppy can't do a lot of damage, due to small teeth and weak jaws, but an older puppy can ruin expensive furniture and carpets. For example, if you allow Simon to bite you when he's little, as he grows, this biting is no longer a play behavior. It turns into a dominant behavior of your dog telling you what to do.

You are setting precedents in Simon's life from the very beginning. Simply don't allow him to do something while he's young that you don't want him to continue doing later. Simon will not hold a grudge against you, nor will he get hurt feelings. Puppies actually become more relaxed and attached to people when they understand their environment. Being consistent from the beginning will accomplish these goals.

There are many stages in a puppy's life. In fact, many scientists believe that dogs go through 15 to 21 human years of behavioral development during their first year. Simon will go through teething, testing, and discovering hierarchy all in his first six months, each presenting different challenges.

Acclimate your puppy to his collar and leash as soon as you take him home and always supervise him when he is outside.

Teething begins at three months and continues until Simon reaches nine months. While Simon may have oral fixations as a 2-month-old pup, it's not until around 12 weeks that his front baby teeth will begin falling out. By 16 weeks, he'll be losing his incisors, and by 5 months, he'll be losing his molars. Throughout this period, new teeth will be coming in, causing much discomfort. Human babies cry; canine babies chew.

You had better watch your furniture, carpets, and molding very carefully. Wood objects in particular, such as table and chair legs, will bear the brunt of sore gums. Instead of having to replace everything you own and blaming your puppy, teach Simon from day one what he can and cannot put his mouth on by watching him closely.

You'll need to provide Simon with a variety of chew toys and keep an eye on him to make sure he chews the appropriate things. A great way of keeping Simon's attention on his own toys is to put Simon's kibble inside hollow toys. Giving your pup most of his meals in this manner for the first three months will ensure that Simon will never touch anything other than his toys. After this period, you can feed him in a dish, and Simon will most likely maintain his fixation on his toys.

When you cannot watch Simon, put him in his crate or an area that is puppy-proofed. This will prevent any mishaps while you are away. Simon will feel more relaxed, and you will be able to rest easy knowing your house will still be in one piece when you return. This also helps reduce separation anxiety. A dog in a den feels protected; a dog loose in an open area feels anxiety. Anxiety can make a puppy destructive.

If you see Simon testing out a chair leg to see if it's as tasty as his chew toy, push him away as you growl at him. Immediately return his attention to his toy by playing with him. This will redirect his attention to something positive, as all puppy training should be.

Make teething a little easier for Simon by offering him ice cubes. If Simon does not like plain ice cubes, freeze some chicken bullion in an ice cube tray and make puppy popsicles. Another teething treat is a moistened, twisted washcloth that has been frozen. Allow Simon to gnaw on the washcloth until it melts. The ideal teething treat is a frozen marrowbone. They are sold at your local grocery store as soup bones with bits of meat and filled with marrow. Not only will Simon go to town on the frozen bone, but also it can be used over and over by adding peanut butter or cheese mixed with his kibble, and freezing it for a future treat.

Testing and hierarchy discovery go hand in hand. Puppies are born with the ability to train their owner. We, on the other hand, have to learn to speak canine in order to properly train our puppy. This means communicating on a very basic principle: the all or none law. Simon can either always do something or never do something.

Dogs don't understand gray areas such as, "It's okay this time, but not next time." For example, Simon jumps on you and you allow it because you're wearing jeans at the time. But what happens when you're dressed for work or for an evening out? Simon doesn't know the difference between nice and casual clothes. All he knows is that if he jumps on you he gets attention. He learned this very quickly when he jumped on you the first time and you petted him. To keep Simon from jumping on you when you wear nice clothes, you'll need to teach him to never jump on you at all.

This task can be especially difficult with friends and family who allow him to jump up. "Oh, he's only a puppy," they say. You must be assertive and tell these people that he must learn to not behave

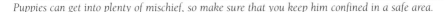

Puppies can get into plenty of mischief, so make sure that you keep him confined in a safe area.

in such a manner. Simon should never receive praise or positive attention when he misbehaves, including placating him by saying, "Oh, it's all right," when he shows fear or aggression. This serves only to reinforce the bad behavior. Always correct the bad behavior by making him do something good, such as sitting and looking up at you for attention instead of jumping. Give him his food only after he sits, not while jumping around. Don't let him outside until he sits first. Don't pet him unless he performs a command for you. This puts you in the top position. Teaching Simon to do as you request before he receives anything maintains your dominance without having to be harsh in any way.

These concepts should be used for everything a puppy can get into, such as raiding the garbage can, jumping on furniture and counters, chewing shoes and towels, digging in the yard, and excessive barking. Saying, "Stop it, stop it," in a placating, soft tone of voice will not cure the problem. You must take charge, whether Simon is a Yorkshire Terrier or a Great Dane. As soon as Simon shows any signs of doing something wrong, correct him immediately by pushing him away, as you growl and redirect his attention onto a toy.

Curing Bad Habits

If Simon has already wrapped you around his paw and has begun to misbehave there are ways to cure the problems in a way he understands. Never hit, yell, swear, or hold grudges because Simon will not understand. Dogs do not behave in this manner. You'll only be causing worse problems, such as fear-biting and submissive urination. Use canine language to make your point. Simon will understand and learn faster, with less confusion.

If you do not want your dog to acquire bad habits, like sleeping on your bed, do not allow him to do so when he is a puppy.

Provide your puppy with lots of toys to chew on to keep both him and your belongings safe.

Jumping

When dogs greet each other, they first touch noses. Initially, Simon is jumping up to say hello. After all, your muzzle is way up in the air. When you pet him at this time, he learns that jumping up earns him attention. He then begins jumping up as a means of demanding your attention. Unless you don't care about going to work with paw prints on your clothing, you should teach Simon that jumping up is not proper behavior.

The easiest teaching method is to not give him attention when he jumps up. You can prevent your dog from jumping up by moving back as his front feet leave the floor. Without you to land on, Simon discovers that jumping up has no benefits, and he will eventually stop the behavior. You do have to have good timing, however, for if Simon does get his paws on you, the correction won't work.

A means of curing a bad jumping problem is to make a "No Jump" box, which has many uses. A "No Jump" box is a small metal can, such as a band-aid box, tea tin, or coffee can. Place 15 pennies inside and close the lid securely. You may want to make two or three "No Jump" boxes and place them strategically near doors, in the kitchen, and in the family room so you're always prepared.

When Simon jumps up, shake the can *hard* in an up-and-down motion, once or twice. You won't need to shake it more than this because the noise burst will make Simon move away. As soon as all

If your puppy seems curious about his surroundings and interested in new things, it may indicate that he will be easy to train.

four of his feet are on the ground, make him sit. Once he's sitting, pat his head and praise him, teaching Simon that good things come to puppies that sit for attention.

Chewing

Puppies are very orally oriented. They will put their mouths on anything, including you. This may be cute while Simon has his little baby teeth, but it will not be cute as his jaw pressure increases. It also turns from Simon exploring his environment into his dominating his environment. This behavior should be stopped immediately.

As soon as Simon puts his mouth on you, take him by the scruff of the neck, look him in his eyes, and growl. Continue to hold him and stare at him until he looks away first. If you look away first, you are giving in to him, regardless of the fact that you are holding him by his scruff. *Never look away first.* Also, be aware that Simon's blinking is an indication of his submission. You can release Simon after a blink or two. Holding him longer would be counterproductive, making him more aggressive.

This correction must be done quickly and firmly or it can backfire on you. If you do this incorrectly, Simon will become more tenacious and start biting on purpose. If you are not comfortable with this procedure, try spraying Bitter Apple™ on your hands just before playing with Simon. He'll hate the taste and immediately let go of your hand. Puppies have fairly good memories and rarely return to something that resulted in a bad experience.

Chewing on household items is a common occurrence as puppies explore their surroundings. At first, they put things in their mouths to see what is edible, not just to chew. As puppies develop and begin to teethe, chewing becomes a form of relief for their sore gums. Unless you want to have to replace your furniture and other items, start teaching Simon which things he can and cannot chew on. Namely, he can chew on his own toys, but not on your belongings. Also, don't give him old things that you really don't care about anymore as toys, including shoes, towels, socks, and stuffed toys. Having no idea what the difference is, Simon may think that the new shoes left by the door are as fun as the ones you gave him.

There are several ways you can correct Simon for chewing inappropriate items. Keep in mind that there will be little need for corrections provided you are always with him when he is outside his enclosure. One way is to use your "No Jump" box to distract him from chewing the bad thing. Growl at Simon as you firmly shake the can up and down once or twice. Present a toy and praise Simon as soon as he puts his mouth on his own toy.

Another way to correct this problem is to do the same procedure as when Simon tried chewing on you. Take him by the scruff of the neck, look him in the eyes, and growl. When he shows submission, let go and turn his attention onto one of his toys. A squeaky stuffed toy would definitely grab his attention. Remember that you must be quick and firm with this correction for it to work.

When dogs show displeasure, their reaction is always quick and firm. As soon as the other dog submits, the correction is over and both dogs are friends again. This is the same approach you should take when training your puppy. Never hold a grudge and always direct, watch, and communicate in a way Simon understands.

Basic Training and Show Training

Regardless of your future activities, Simon requires basic training. He must know how to come when you call him, sit, lay down, and stay. These are the building blocks of all training. Once learned, you can easily teach him the nuances of other behaviors, such as fetching the newspaper or playing Frisbee™.

Begin each training session by having Simon target. Targeting is a means of obtaining his attention and preparing him for learning new behaviors. In fact, he'll easily learn how to sit within the first couple minutes of the targeting exercise. Targeting is the basis of operant conditioning. Most animals are trained through operant conditioning; even rats and pigeons used in learning studies. Essentially, operant conditioning consists of receiving a reward for producing a correct response. Through breaking a behavior down into smaller sections, dogs can easily learn how to eventually perform the entire behavior within a short period of time without any negative associations.

Target and Sit

This exercise will teach Simon to stop whatever he is doing, remain still, and pay attention. This is very important, because your puppy can't learn if you do not first obtain his interest. Simon will learn the target and sit exercise within a few minutes. Yes, puppies *do* learn that fast.

Begin your first training session by giving Simon a treat and saying, "Good" as he takes it from you. Do this several times. Next, hold the treat in your fingers, place your hand within his reach, and wait for him to touch your hand with his nose. Say, "Good, dog!" and give him the treat. Repeat this two or three times.

Next, move your hand a little to the left and then the right. As Simon keeps his nose on target, praise him and give him a treat. Add an up-and-down motion while you continue to praise Simon for performing correctly by following your hand. Each time Simon follows the target reward him.

Now we'll teach Simon to sit. Place your targeting hand in front of your pup's nose and lift it slightly upward toward his eyes. As you do this say, "Simon, Sit." Your pup will be watching his target, and as his head moves upward, his rear end will go down, like a seesaw. The moment Simon's rear end touches the ground, praise him and give him a reward.

Come and Sit

One of the most important things your puppy can ever do for you is to come when called. Your puppy is very insecure until he reaches the age of five months and, therefore, will easily learn this behavior. He'll want to be near you at all times, so when you move away, he'll automatically follow you.

Put your targeting hand under your pup's nose. Let Simon smell the treat. Step backward two to three steps as you say, "Simon, Come," in a happy, positive tone of voice. Simon will immediately follow his target. Praise him enthusiastically *as* he comes toward you. Don't wait to praise when he arrives. It's important to let him know how good he is the entire time he is behaving properly.

When he stops, bring your hand over his head to an area just between his eyes so that he must look upward. Be sure your hand is not more than two inches from his nose or he'll likely jump up.

Even the youngest puppy has a great capacity to learn whatever you may want to teach him. These two pups practice their sit.

While he's looking up say, "Simon, Sit." As soon as his rear end goes down, praise him and give him a treat.

Continually increase your steps backward as you do the come command so Simon will learn to come from increasingly longer distances. Always make him sit when he arrives. The last thing you want Simon to learn is to come and then leave, or to come and jump up. A come and sit maintains his attention on you while teaching him appropriate behavior patterns.

Once Simon is reliably coming and sitting, attach a lightweight leash (anywhere from four to six feet in length) to his regular neck collar. Let him drag the leash while you work with him. This will acclimate Simon to the feeling of the leash without having it pulled or used in a manner that

Proper socialization is the key to a well-adjusted and well-behaved dog. Your new puppy should meet as many people as possible.

he does not understand. Don't allow children to pull on his leash at this time. All associations with the leash must be positive for Simon to *want* to learn.

Round Robin

When Simon is able to come and sit, it's time to involve the entire family. First, everyone must do the come and sit exercises with him individually so that he learns to listen to everyone. Simon must learn that he is to be Omega dog (the bottom of the hierarchy) in the pack. The last thing you want is for a dog that listens only to one family member and ignores and takes advantage of the other family members. This can cause a rift in the family.

Two family members should stand about six feet apart, facing each other. These are the positions for the Round Robin game. The Round Robin game is the fundamental means of teaching your puppy how to perform specific behaviors such as sit, stay, down, and come, through puppy play.

This type of training has many benefits. First, your puppy has a great time, thus maintaining a longer attention span. He will also learn to work for everyone in the family, not just one person. Third, your pup will become very tired, needing several hours of rest afterward. A tired puppy stays out of trouble, giving you peace of mind for a while.

Begin by calling Simon to come. As soon as he sits and receives his treat, the next person calls him. Simon will come to each of you in turn and sit facing you. Go back and forth a few times, and then increase the distance by taking one big step backward while the other person has Simon's attention. You can continue increasing the distance up to about 30 feet. More than that would be too much on Simon's little puppy legs.

If Simon becomes distracted during his travels between family members, the person who last called him should try to regain his attention by putting a treat under Simon's nose. If this is not enough, then that person should take hold of the leash and gently bring Simon to the other family member. This is very important, for Simon will quickly figure out whose voice has meaning and whose does not. Dogs will not listen to those who do not back up their commands.

Heel and Sit

The Round Robin come and sit exercises will easily be transferred into the heel and sit work. Simon already knows most of it. He knows to follow the target and that when he arrives at it, he must sit. All you have to do is transfer your target to your left side instead of holding it in front of your. Simon will then go to your left side and sit; his quivering nose reaching for a treat.

Begin the exercise by having Simon come and sit. As soon as he sits, place yourself at his right side, your left leg even with his shoulder. This is the proper heeling position. It is important that Simon learns to remain in this position, otherwise he cannot be attentive. Once at Simon's side, maintain his attention by keeping your target on your left leg at knee level. When his nose targets on your hand, offer a reward as you praise him. Once he's finished with the treat say, "Simon, Heel," and take a step forward on your left leg. Moving your left leg first becomes Simon's visual cue for the heel command. He'll learn to move forward as your leg moves forward. This reaction is very normal and, in most dogs, automatic.

Your pup must learn to walk nicely on a leash for his safety and for the safety of others.

Go only one step and stop. Simon will most likely follow his target and move forward with you. As soon as he does, give him praise. When you stop, say, "Simon, Sit." As soon as he sits, give him the treat. Keep increasing your steps each time you do the heel exercise. Within a short time you and Simon will be walking 5, 10, 20 steps or more. Once you get this far you can begin incorporating turns. Do a turn to the right and stop directly after the turn. This will keep Simon at your side. During later training, executing turns will be the best means of maintaining Simon's attention. Right turns will help keep Simon from running in front of you and sniffing, while left turns will maintain the exact proper heel position and teach Simon to watch you better.

If, at any time, Simon becomes disenchanted by his target and more interested in the last rock he passed, place the reward under his nose and draw him closer to you. Decrease the amount of steps between your start and stop. Maybe his current reward is not inviting enough, so try something else. If he was interested in that rock, maybe holding it would maintain his attention. The reward does not always have to be food. Some dogs prefer tennis balls or Frisbees™.

Another thing you can do to maintain his interest once he's gotten pretty good at heeling is to change your pace now and then. Simon must learn to remain at your side whether you are walking slow or fast. In fact, one of the

Although this Petit Basset Griffon Vendeen puppy doesn't seem to mind, the down command may be hard for some puppies to accept because it puts them in a submissive position.

ways to obtain the attention of a distracted pup is to jog. Most pups will eagerly run after a fast-moving playmate. Just don't let him think you're a puppy playmate, for Simon must always know that you're the pack leader. Do any pace change in short bursts, and always praise Simon as he catches up with you. Should he overshoot, turn to the right and lure him back to your side with the bait.

Down

The next command on your training agenda is the down. This is initially taught during the Round Robin game. It should be interspersed with the sit command. For example, on one round Simon sits and the next round Simon sits and then lies down before the next person calls him.

The down can sometimes be difficult to teach because it is a submissive position. If Simon has a dominant personality, he will not easily learn the down command. However, this is even more reason to begin teaching him this behavior as early as you can. While your puppy is young, he is less apt to test his pack position then when he reaches the more independent age of 18 to 20 weeks. An older, dominant puppy will not go down, even for a special treat. He'll have to be trained using a more formal method that involves placing him into position.

Targeting is the easiest means of teaching Simon to down on his own. Place the treat between your thumb and middle finger. When Simon arrives and sits, let him smell the treat as you point down at the ground between his front toes. His head will dip downward. Most puppies will follow their heads and bring the rest of their bodies down as well. If your particular puppy does not do so on his own, apply gentle pressure on his shoulder blades. He should easily drop on his belly. As soon as he is lying down, give him lots of praise and his treat.

Be absolutely certain to vary your request for the down. This is very important, for you don't want Simon to believe that he arrives and lies down. He should always come and sit first, and await his next command.

Dogs are easily pattern trained. If you repeat something as few as three times, Simon will learn the pattern and tend to anticipate your commands. While it's nice to know Simon really wants to please you that much, it does not mean that he's obedience trained. Change around the sit and down and even mix the heeling into your requests. Keep Simon guessing and attentive.

Stay

The next command Simon will learn is the stay. This can be the most difficult thing for a puppy to learn. Young dogs are constantly in motion. Remaining still in the same spot is not on the top of their agenda. The stay command will need to be done through successive approximation, a gradual increase one step at a time.

Successive approximation was used when you began teaching Simon to heel by taking one step and then two steps. As he accomplished a couple steps, you went on to more steps in between each

Every puppy can benefit from basic obedience training. A well-trained puppy will be welcomed anywhere.

stop and sit. Before long you were walking ten steps and doing turns. You successively increased the criterion for each ultimate reward—the treat.

Begin teaching the stay exercise by first playing the Round Robin game. When Simon arrives and sits, place the palm of your hand in front of his nose and say, "Simon, Stay." Hold the treat, near his nose but don't give it to him for three to five seconds. Praise him as he remains in place. Give him a treat and then the next person should call him to come. Each time you have him come and sit, increase the amount of time Simon *has* to maintain a stay before receiving his reward.

Since you'll have a lot to do within a short time frame, looking at your watch is not something you can coordinate with making sure your pup remains sitting. You can more easily count the seconds by using "Good, boy" One second equals one "Good, boy." The first time you do a stay you'll say, "Good, boy," one or two times. The next time, Simon gets two or three and

Praise, play, and affection are the best training motivators for your puppy.

so on, until Simon can remain in place at least 30 seconds.

By the time you reach five to six words of praise, Simon may start popping up and trying to go to the next person. You can prevent this by stepping on his leash when he arrives and sits before you. If he gets up, you can easily bring him back into position and repeat your stay command. After placing him back in the same location, again tell him to stay, only this time shorten the amount of time to two or three, "Good, boys." Sometimes you need to regress in order to progress. When working a puppy, everything needs to remain as positive as possible. Go back to a comfortable zone—less time in the stay. Keeping a positive attitude increases Simon's desire to please you.

Each time you have a training session, increase your pup's stay time. In a few weeks, he'll be able to remain in one spot for up to 45 seconds without any problem. Practice the stay exercise with the down position as well. Remember to vary all the exercises in order to keep Simon attentive.

When Simon is able to remain in the sit/stay for 30 seconds, it is time to introduce the next variable—moving around him as he remains sitting. This needs to be done with a gradual increase of movement. You begin by stepping side to side while you face your puppy. The next time you do a

Training for conformation takes preparation and dedication, but most of all, it should be enjoyable for both the dogs and the handlers.

stay command, you step on either side of him, from his head to his back legs on both sides. As Simon remains sitting throughout your motion, you can begin doing a complete circle around him.

Always replace your puppy *every* time he gets up. He must be replaced as close to the original location where you told him to perform his sit/stay as possible. This way he learns to remain where you told him to stay, not where he chooses to stay. Allowing Simon to pop up and then sit where he chooses will not teach him to stay.

As Simon accepts your walking around him, try doing so in both directions. Then, begin to increase your distance as you move around him. Add a foot or two of space between you and Simon each time you do a sit/stay. Within several training sessions, you should be able to get six feet away from him as he remains in his sit/stay. Go around him in both directions so that he doesn't become accustomed to your moving in only one direction.

Practice this exercise with the down/stay as well. The only difference will be that instead of your stepping in front of Simon, you'll begin your side to side movements along his right side and proceed to walk around him by going around his back end first. This way, Simon is less likely to get up.

Conformation Preparation

Most dog handlers who show their pups in conformation do not want a puppy to even know the meaning of sit until they have obtained their championship points. While this can be helpful in the ring, you must also think about how this will affect Simon's in-home behavior. A dog that cannot sit on command will also have difficulty with stay and down, as well as general obedience. If you obtained Simon as primarily a conformation dog, and he lives in a kennel with little in-home time, then by all means don't teach him sit. Had you obtained Simon first and foremost as a pet and secondly as a conformation dog, then you must teach him to sit.

A conformation dog will not only need to learn how to stack (stand/stay), but also learn to prance in front of you instead of at your side, as an obedience-trained dog must. Also, the prancing dog cannot be jumping around or dragging you behind him. A long, consistent strut is preferred.

In order to obtain the best scores and decrease the amount of time required to obtain that elusive conformation championship, you may want to hire a professional handler. The handler will know how to properly exhibit your dog to his best advantage.

However, you can still help your handler by teaching your dog to stack before sending him into the circuit.

1. While you are walking your dog, place the entire leash into your right hand.
2. Bring your left hand along the right side of Simon's body from his nose to his hip,
3. Put your left hand under his tummy and apply gentle pressure as you stop and say, "Simon, Stand."
4. Rub his tummy for a few seconds and then take him forward again.

Repeat this exercise often and gradually increase the amount of time Simon remains standing with you rubbing his tummy. When your puppy relaxes into the stand/stay position, gradually decrease the amount of pressure against his tummy and begin moving your hands over his body.

With proper training, who knows what your little puppy can accomplish? If your puppy enjoys obedience, you can teach him to participate in more advanced dog sports like agility.

Massage his legs, abdomen, and neck. Move your hands onto his head and practice lifting his ears, looking into his eyes, and lifting his lips so that you can see his teeth. All these things prepare him for a judges' examination. Once you can touch Simon all over and he can remain standing steady throughout, ask other people to do the same. The more people, especially those who don't know Simon, you can get to touch him, the better.

To teach Simon to strut in front of you, try using a toy or treat that he likes. When you wish him to step out, throw the toy/treat about ten feet in front of him. Allow him to go after the reward and praise him when he does so. He should always be quick to return to your side and walk with you, however. You don't want a dog that's always pulling on you. Within a short period of time you can hold the reward in your right hand, the leash in your left, and use the reward as bait to get him moving forward. The reward can also be used to get Simon to perk his ears forward and lift his head while in a stacking position, just by showing it to him while he maintains a stand/stay. A squeaky toy is ideal for this purpose. All you need to do is squeak it and he perks up.

Preparation for Frisbee™, Flyball, and Agility

All dogs going into these sports must first be obedience trained both on and off leash, and second, must know how to retrieve, jump, and solve problems. Having Simon work well off leash while surrounded by distractions is of supreme importance. The best way of achieving this goal is to practice with him in different places around various distractions. However, you cannot begin with this until he has learned all of his basic obedience work and will consistently perform on one command.

Once you have completed puppy kindergarten, the next logical step is to join a class where Simon will learn more formal work while surrounded by other dogs and people. This will also offer him some much needed socialization time. A socialized puppy is friendly, outgoing, and rarely nervous while competing.

Some puppies will automatically want to chase tennis balls and Frisbees™, while others ignore these things. Save yourself lots of heartache and do not force your puppy to retrieve something that does not interest him. A pup that naturally goes after the Frisbee™ and tennis ball will probably be easily trained into a Frisbee™ or flyball dog. One that does not might prefer agility work, where he must learn to negotiate various obstacles.

The PAT test discussed earlier will help you decide which type of pup you have. There are more types of competition than space to discuss them. Choose an activity that best suits the breed and personality of your dog. This will ensure a long-lasting and fun relationship with your purebred puppy.

Index

Photo Credits

All photographs by Isabelle Francais.